People of the Caves

GREAT STORY & COOL FACTS

Introduction

Welcome to Half and Half books, a great combination of story and facts! You might want to read this book on your own. However, the section with real facts is a little more difficult to read than the story. You might find it helpful to read the facts section with your parent, or someone else, who can help you with the more difficult words. Your parent may also be able to answer any questions you have about the facts—or at least help you find more information!

People of the Caves

English Edition translated by Wendy Helfenbaum and edited by Editorial Services of Los Angeles and Sindy McKay

Original Edition: Ton ancêtre Cro-Magnon

The Almost Wolf by Alain Surget
Illustrated by François Avril

Non-fiction text by Julien Hirsinger
Non-fiction illustrations by Marc Botta and Jean-Pierre Duffour
Activity by Béatrice Garel

Photography Credits
A. Hodel/AKG Paris; F. Gohier/Explorer; A. Glory/collection of Musée de l'Homme; C. and J. Lenars/Explorer; A. Marshack/ coll. Musée de l'Homme; ,Delaplanche/ coll. Musée de l'Homme.; coll. Musée de l'Homme; J. Oster/ coll. Musée de l'Homme; R.M.N.; Larivière/ coll. Musée de l'Homme; J. Oster/ coll. Musée de l'Homme; P. Tetrel/Explorer.; J. Oster/ coll. Musée de l'Homme.; D. Ponsard/ coll. Musée de l'Homme.; F. Gohier/Explorer; J. Oster/ coll. Musée de l'Homme; R.G. Ojeda/R.M.N.; J. Oster/ coll. Musée de l'Homme. Photography for Activity: F. Hanoteau/Nathan.

Special thanks to Martine Houmeau-Borda.

Published by Treasure Bay, Inc.
40 Sir Francis Drake Boulevard
San Anselmo, CA 94960 USA

PRINTED IN SINGAPORE

Library of Congress Catalog Card Number: 2008920815

Hardcover ISBN-13: 978-1-60115-205-3
Paperback ISBN-13: 978-1-60115-206-0

Visit us online at:
www.HalfAndHalfBooks.com

People of the Caves

Table of Contents

Story: The Almost Wolf

Facts: The Cro-Magnon People

The Almost Wolf

Story by **Alain Surget**
Illustrated by **François Avril**

1

The Chief's Son

The night sky above was a deep, rich blue and the full moon shone like a huge, round eye. Down below, a fire burned in front of a cave. Around the fire sat the cave people, eating their evening meal. As they ate, they smacked their lips and licked their fingers clean.

Suddenly the chief of the tribe stopped eating and looked around. "Where is Roe?" he growled. "Where is my son?"

The members of the tribe looked at their large, strong chief and shrugged. No one had seen Roe.

"Roe has the spirit of a moth," said the medicine man. "He dreams by the light of the moon."

"It would be better for Roe to have the spirit of a boar," said his father. "He should be thinking more about hunting and less about the stars."

"He's only ten years old," pointed out Roe's mother.

"At his age, I was already running after reindeer!" said the chief, frowning. "I'm going to go and find him!"

The tribe watched as the chief stomped away with his club in his hand. They were frightened for Roe, for their chief was clearly very angry.

Not far away, under the bright light of the moon, young Roe lay on his belly in the grass. Lying beside him was his best friend, Mae. Roe did not know his father was looking for him. He was too busy watching a large wolf as it moved to the edge of a nearby cliff. The wolf was quickly joined by another. Before long, an entire pack of wolves was gathered in the clear moonlight.

Roe and Mae watched the wolf pack for a moment. Then Mae pointed to a different cliff and cried out, "Look! There's another pack of wolves!"

The two packs faced each other. "Wooooo!" One pack began to sing, snouts lifted toward the moon and stars.

Roe and Mae waited for the second pack to answer. But instead, they remained as silent as the rocks they stood on.

"Why aren't they singing?" asked Mae. "Wolves always sing at the full moon!"

Roe scratched his head, thinking. "Maybe they're almost like wolves, but not real wolves," he replied.

Before Mae could answer, they heard the sound of heavy footsteps approaching.

"Something's coming!" hissed Roe. "It could be a bear or a saber-tooth tiger!"

Quickly the two friends raced to a big rock and huddled behind it. They hardly dared to breathe as the footsteps grew louder. Then, suddenly the footsteps stopped.

After a moment, Roe bravely peeked out.

"What is it?" asked Mae fearfully.

Roe stood and sheepishly said, "It's my father."

The chief loomed tall in front of his son, shaking his head in disapproval. "Still hearing a wolf's howl as a song of the night, I see. When will you learn that those howls are simply the way wolves call to one another as they prepare for a hunt?"

"Chief?" began Mae in a small voice.

"Silence!" thundered the chief.

Then, he turned to face Roe again. "Son, I want you to become a great warrior, a great hunter, and a great stone carver. But you spend your days observing ants. You waste your time studying the flight of birds. And when you carve a stone, it looks more like the head of a baby than the head of a spear."

"But Chief . . ." repeated Mae.

"Silence!"

Mae cowered a bit as the chief continued talking to his son.

"One day, you will become chief of this tribe, Roe, and you will need to know how to do many things. Tomorrow the wolves will lead us to a bison herd. You will come with us. It will be your first hunt. It is time you learn how to find food."

"Chief!" insisted Mae again.

The chief shot Mae a warning look and she was quiet. Then he hissed to his son, "What do you have to say for yourself?"

Roe blinked up at his father. "Why are the wolves in one pack singing and the others are not?"

The chief was surprised by the question. "What?! I don't know. Maybe they've bitten off their own tongues! Now let's go home."

"CHIEF!" This time, Mae grabbed him by the arm.

"What is it that you want, Mae?!"

"I just wanted to tell you, Great Chief, that you have stepped with both feet into a pile of bison dung."

Standing behind his father, Roe covered his grinning mouth with his hand.

2

The Hunt

Late that night, the dying embers of the fire crackled in front of the cave. The men of the tribe danced around it, their chests and faces painted red. They shook their spears and leaped over the flames, preparing for tomorrow's hunt. "Ooah, ooah!" they chanted! For the first time, Roe danced and chanted with them.

The women clapped their hands, encouraging the men with their cries. The children watched their fathers with admiring eyes. How they would love to be older and be able to go with them on the hunt!

At the chief's signal, the cave people plunged pieces of wood into the fire. Using them as torches to light up the night sky, the men and boys ran toward the end of the cave.

There, the medicine man had painted a large bison on the wall. One after another, the hunters hit the drawing with their weapons. This was to show what they would do when they found the real animal tomorrow. The cave people believed that this play-acting would give them good luck and help them on their hunt.

Roe threw his spear at the wall. It missed and hit a bearskin that was drying out instead. "Ouch!" cried Roe as the spear bounced back and hit him in the shoulder.

"Don't worry," his father assured him. "When you see the real bison in front of you, you will not miss your target."

As the men left the cave, the sound of an old woman's voice was heard complaining behind them, "A brand new skin! That boy tore a brand new skin!"

Early the next morning, the cave people followed the wolves to a herd of bison.

The bison somehow sensed the coming danger and a large male lifted his head to bellow out a cry of alarm. The others stopped grazing. The females hurriedly gathered their young in close.

The wolves approached and slowly surrounded the hairy beasts. Then leader of the wolf pack rushed in, setting off the attack.

The bison stampeded in a flurry of hooves!

"They're headed in our direction!" rejoiced Roe's father. He quickly ordered some of his hunters to spear the bison, while the others were to drive the wolves away.

“Come with me!” the chief shouted to his son.

Roe followed his father. Together, they stood watch from behind a rock, waiting for the stampeding bison to pass by them.

The first beasts arrived. Hunters came out of the tall grass to scare off the wolves and the wolves abandoned the chase. Then several spears whistled through the air, landing in the flanks of bison. There would be meat for the tribe tonight!

A large male bison split from the rest of the herd.

“There!” the chief shouted to Roe. “That’s the one for you. Use my spear. It’s stronger than yours!”

The beast galloped toward them with his head down. Roe raised his weapon, closed his eyes, and threw the spear with all his might.

With a simple tilt of the head, the bison ducked the spear. It splintered into pieces against a large rock.

Furious now, the animal set his sights on the young hunter. He charged right toward him and Roe quickly dove behind a rock! "Run, father, run!" he shouted to the chief.

With no spear to defend himself, the chief took his son's advice. He began to run!

Suddenly, the chief slipped on some mud! He flew up into the air and came down to land in the mud with a splat! The bison thundered past him and ran away.

Aside from having the wind knocked out of him, the chief was fine. The other hunters rushed up to the chief. Upon seeing him spread out like a starfish, all covered in mud, one of the hunters burst out laughing. The others looked at him with surprise.

They had never heard laughter before. They tried to imitate the sound and found it gave them a pleasant feeling. Soon, all of the men were laughing.

The chief wanted to be angry, but this wonderful new sound made him smile instead. As the hunters helped him to his feet, the chief even laughed a bit himself.

3

The Wolf That Did Not Howl

That night, back at the cave, the tribe celebrated a successful hunt. The hunters told the story of how their chief had been chased by a bison and had slipped in the mud. The medicine man drew the funny scene on a wall. The tribe laughed to see how silly their fierce chief had looked today.

Roe, however, was not laughing. He was not allowed to be part of the festivities. All he was given to eat was one piece of old boiled meat, as hard as wood. The chief had sent his son away from the group, saying, "You will not have any fresh meat until you make yourself useful to this tribe."

As Roe sat pouting, Mae appeared and handed him a piece of freshly roasted bison.

"Take it," she said. "It's better than chewing on that piece of old leather your father gave you."

Roe bit eagerly into the delicious, juicy meat.

Suddenly, Mae was quiet. Something was stirring in the bushes. Both children stopped breathing as the bushes parted and out walked an animal.

"A wolf!" gasped Mae, as she jumped up to run away.

Roe held her back. "No," he murmured. "It's one of those creatures that doesn't howl."

The beast stood in front of them, on guard. It was carefully watching their movements and growling softly.

Roe still had the hard piece of meat that his father had given him. He placed the meat on his palm and slowly stretched out his hand toward the animal's nose.

The animal stopped growling.

The almost-wolf stretched his nose toward the meat, sniffing. The smell was tempting, but the animal clearly did not trust Roe and Mae.

Mae held her breath. Her heart was pounding so hard that she thought she was hearing the drums before a hunting feast. What if this almost-wolf decided to bite off Roe's fingers along with the meat?

Mae wanted the animal to leave, but her young friend was still patiently holding out the meat to it. The almost-wolf backed up and circled around the children. Then it came back to stop once again in front of Roe's hand.

Roe's fears disappeared. If the almost-wolf had wanted to bite him, it would have done so already.

Roe wiggled his fingers, inviting the almost-wolf to come closer.

Chomp!

With one quick snap of its jaw, the animal grabbed up the meat and gulped it down. Then it came back to sniff Roe's hand. It smelled the leftover scent of the meat and began to lick Roe's fingers.

Mae's face broke into a smile.

Roe liked the way she pulled up the corners of her mouth when she was happy. He thought it made her look very attractive.

Roe smiled back at her.

"It seems like the almost-wolf is happy, too," Mae remarked. "I've never seen an animal wagging its tail like that!"

Mae dared to put out her hand to touch the animal's coat. It felt rough and soft at the same time.

The almost-wolf was startled by her touch, but soon let her slide her fingers down its back. It even let her tickle it under the chin, where the fur was extra soft. It was the first time the almost-wolf had felt the joy of being petted.

Roe and Mae returned to the cave with the almost-wolf following behind. The tribe was stunned to see them. The men gripped their weapons and the children hid behind their mothers.

"Your son has tamed a wolf!" gasped the medicine man.

After a moment of surprise, the chief welcomed his son with open arms.

"No one has dared to do what you have done today. You have tamed a fearsome beast," the chief said proudly. "This animal will stay with us. We will feed it and it will help us find the tracks of our prey."

The chief raised his voice and spoke proudly to the tribe, "I always knew that one day my son would astonish us!"

Mae smiled at her best friend, happy to see him basking in his father's pride.

Then the chief turned back to Roe and said, "It is up to you now to name this almost-wolf, my son."

"How about . . . dog?" said Roe.

"Dog it shall be!" declared the chief.

And from that day on, dog became Roe's best friend. Rather, his second best friend—after Mae, of course.

A New People Appear

More than 40,000 years ago, Cro-Magnon people arrived in Europe. Evidence seems to indicate that the ancestors of the Cro-Magnon people originally came from Africa. When the Cro-Magnons arrived, there was a type of primitive people, called Neanderthals, still living in Europe. Over time, the Cro-Magnons replaced the Neanderthals, who were gradually disappearing.

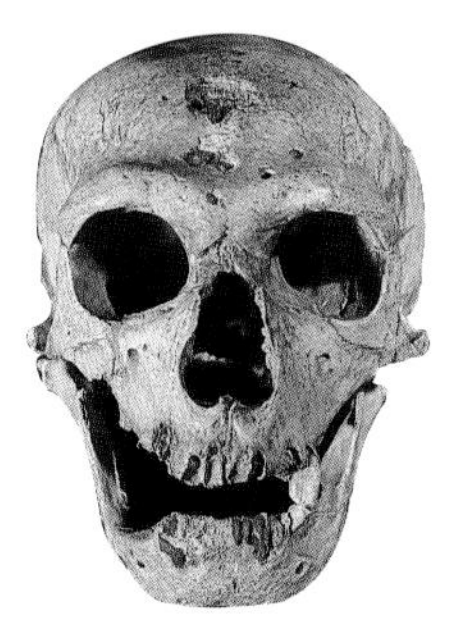

Neanderthal Skull

Cro-Magnon Skull

While the Cro-Magnons lived a long time ago, they were humans, very much like us. They are called Cro-Magnons because the first skeletons were found under the Cro-Magnon rock, in Dordogne, France.

A Cro-Magnon human looked much like a modern human.

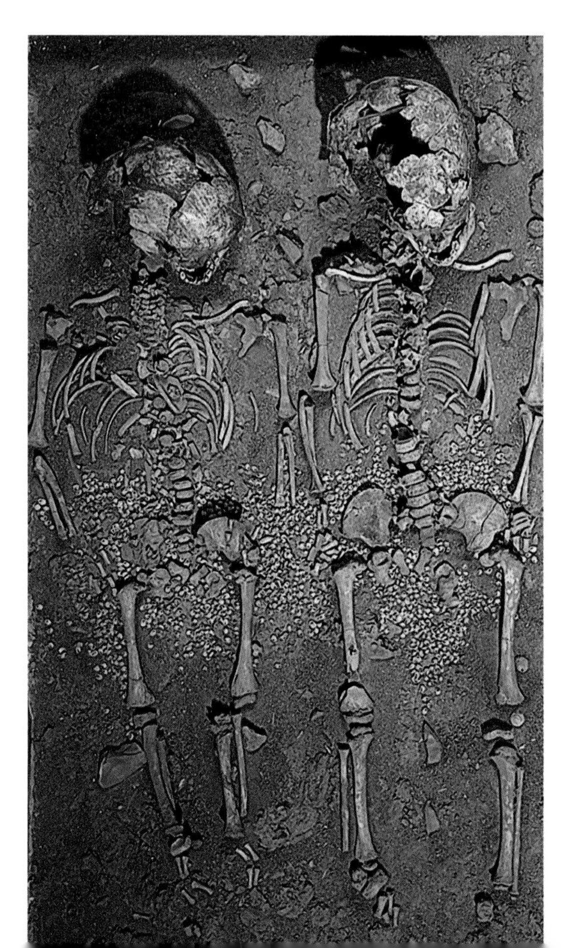

Cro-Magnons were tall. The skeletons that were found generally surpassed five and a half feet in height. Their foreheads were straight and their skulls were bulky. In fact, only their forearms, which were a tiny bit longer than ours, allow us to distinguish them from today's modern people.

A Difficult Life

During much of the time that Cro-Magnon people lived, glaciers occupied northern Europe. Even in the summer, in the warmest areas, the temperature rarely rose above 60 degrees. The Cro-Magnons had to learn to survive in cold weather.

Exposed to the cold, the Cro-Magnon people were confronted with illness and frostbite. Broken bones were common, but evidence exists that suggests that Cro-Magnons may have known how to treat them. However, most Cro-Magnon people did not live very long; they lived only 20 to 40 years.

Herds of reindeer and bison roamed freely in vast open spaces. Competing for this same food were wolves, hyenas, and lions. Cro-Magnons had to be careful to avoid these dangerous creatures.

The Cro-Magnon people faced many dangers.

A Community of Hunters

The Cro-Magnons' diet consisted of food they got from both hunting and gathering. Gathered food included grain, wild carrots, beets, onions, turnips, and other foods they picked and dug. They ate wild game and smaller meats that they hunted. Overall, they had a very well balanced diet.

Evidence suggests that Cro-Magnons may have captured large animals by driving them backward with lit torches toward steep cliffs. Frightened, the animals would fall off the cliffs. Then, all that the Cro-Magnons had to do was climb down to the bottom and pick up their kill.

To kill their prey without getting too close, Cro-Magnon hunters mostly used wooden spears with ivory or flint points. The spears' length and shape were good for precise aiming. A hunter had to be strong, fast, and have good coordination to succeed.

The first concern of the Cro-Magnons was obtaining food.

In addition to hunting larger animals, it is believed that Cro-Magnon people built traps to catch smaller animals such as marmots, beavers, and partridges.

The Cro-Magnon people, like people today, looked for the best locations for shelter. They often lived in or near caves.

The life of Cro-Magnons centered around the fire.

The fire allowed them to get warm, to light their surroundings, to cook, and to smoke the food in order to preserve it longer.

Around the Fire

On long hunts, the Cro-Magnon people built shelters with large tents made of animal skins. They could then move quickly to follow the path of whatever game they were tracking. Some tribes used giant mammoth bones to construct their camp tents.

The Battle of the Bison, painting
40,000–30,000 years ago

Deep in the Caves

Woman Blowing a Horn sculpture
About 20,000 years ago

Bison, engraving
30,000–15,000 years ago

Aurochs, painting
About 15,000 years ago

Man Injured by a Bison, painting
About 15,000 years ago

Ivory Horse, sculpture
35,000–30,000 years ago

Ibex, sculpture
19,000 years ago

Great Inventions

The Cro-Magnons and other groups of early humans perfected flint sharpening and tools. They created the fish hook to go fishing. And they used animal fat in oil lamps to provide light in dark caves.

Our ancestors made advances in many areas.

A Scraper

The hunt provided meat, but equally important, it supplied animal skins. The skins were carefully cut, then cleaned by removing fat with the help of a scraper. They were then dried and tanned to make them waterproof.

A Needle

It then became necessary to invent the needle, carved out of a reindeer bone. Instead of thread, Cro-Magnon people used horsehair. These sewn skins made clothing, shelter, blankets, water bottles, shoes, and more.

Clothes made from skins

The remains of a flute

Cro-Magnon people, like people today, had needs beyond the basic ones of food, clothing, and shelter. Entertainment and learning were probably important in their lives. Using animal bones, they made small flutes. Such flutes may have been used to make music or even to call birds.

Prehistoric Art

Cro-Magnon people painted with the colors yellow, red, and maroon. Many paintings have been discovered deep inside caves. These caves have protected the paintings for thousands of years.

It appears that the painters and the engravers often used the existing bumps and cracks in the cave walls to help them with their art. Some of these bumps may have suggested the shape of an animal, and the artists worked with that shape as they painted or carved.

Carving
About 17,000 years ago

The Cro-Magnon people invented Art as we know it today.

Archeologists have found many pieces of jewelry dating from the time of the Cro-Magnon people: pendants, necklaces made of shells and animal teeth, and bracelets. These treasures were sometimes discovered in tombs.

The most well known paintings are of bison, reindeer, bears, horses, rhinoceroses, and mammoths.

Watch Out for Mistakes!

Modern humans are related to cave people . . .

The Cro-Magnons were a group of early prehistoric humans. People of today are descendents of early prehistoric humans, but are not descendents of Neanderthals.

Here are some facts about the Cro-Magnon people.

Cro-Magnons could not make fire with two pieces of flint . . .

The spark was too weak. He had to scrape the flint against pyrite, which contains sulfur, just as matches do.

Cro-Magnons never saw any dinosaurs . . .

Dinosaurs disappeared 65 million years before the appearance of the first modern human.

Cro-Magnons could do more than simply grunt . . .

Many scientists suspect that Cro-Magnons had some kind of verbal language. It would have been almost impossible to hunt in packs, travel or transmit techniques without communicating with his companions.

Do You Know?

Cro-Magnons came from:

Africa?
America?
Germany?

Africa.

Cro-Magnons could capture their prey thanks to:

A spear?
A wheel?
A canon?

A spear.

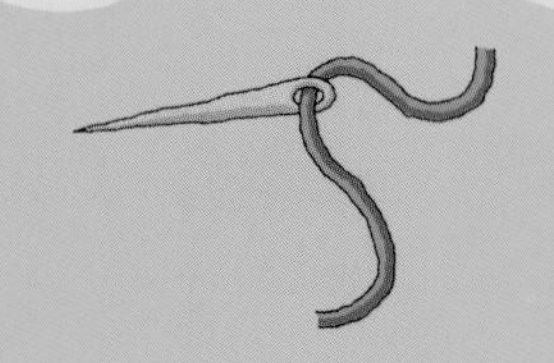

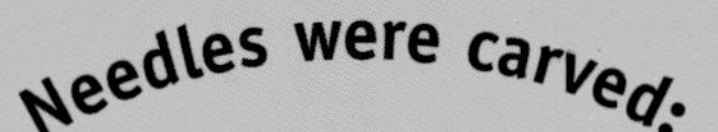

Needles were carved:

Out of rock?
Out of reindeer bones?
Out of human bones?

They were carved out of reindeer bones.

Cro-Magnons played:

The bass guitar?
The flute?
The violin?

A flute.

True or False?

Paintings drawn by the Cro-Magnon people were found on parchment.

False. They were found on walls deep inside caves.

Cro-Magnons cultivated corn.

True or False?

False. Cro-Magnons did not have farms. They gathered grains and vegetables they found.

One of the colors they painted with was:

Green?
Yellow?
Purple?

Yellow.

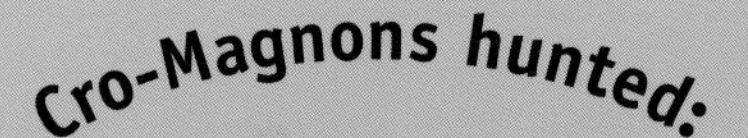

Dinosaurs?
Hyenas?
Unicorns?

They hunted hyenas.

Making what the Cro-Magnons made...

A POSITIVE RELIEF HAND

Dilute the paint with a little water in the plate. Place your hand in the paint, then on the sandpaper. Press down. Then lift up your hand. Done!

For these activities, you will need:

An adult's help and permission, some sheets of sandpaper, maroon non-toxic paint, a straw, a glass, and a paper plate.

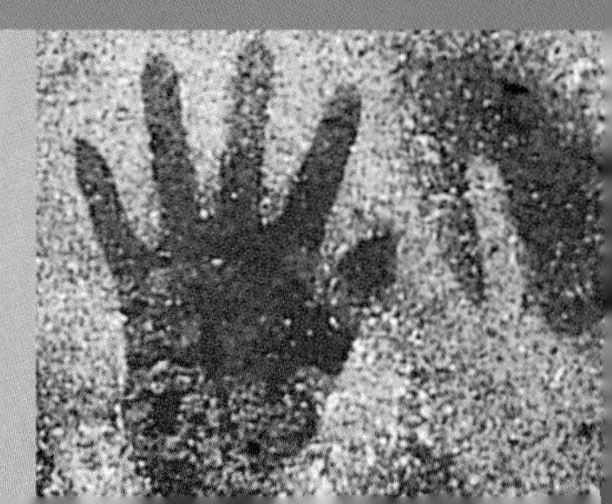

A NEGATIVE RELIEF HAND

Dilute paint in a glass with a little water. Dip a straw into the paint. Place your hand on the sandpaper. Blow the paint around your hand with the straw; do not lift your hand until you are done creating the color around your fingers and palm. Done!

If you liked ***People of the Caves,*** here is another Half and Half™ book you are sure to enjoy!

Get a great story and cool facts about ancient Egypt!

In the story, a young girl wants to go with her father to see the building of the pyramids. Her father leaves without her, saying it is no place for a young girl. Then, she notices something important he left behind. Facing dangers she did not expect, she sets out to find her father—and also see the creation of one of the greatest wonders of the world.

After the story, you can see for yourself how people lived long ago in this ancient land. Plus, find out more about the amazing pyramids they built—and how the mummies of their great Pharaoh kings were buried in those pyramids!

To see all the Half and Half books that are available, just go online to **www.HalfAndHalf.com**